Basher Science

FORENSICS

KINGFISHER
LONDON & NEW YORK

KINGFISHER
LONDON & NEW YORK

Text and design copyright © Toucan Books Ltd. 2023
Illustrations copyright © Simon Basher 2023
www.basherscience.com

First published 2023 in the United States by Kingfisher
120 Broadway, New York, NY 10271
Kingfisher is an imprint of Macmillan Children's Books, London
All rights reserved.

Author: Tom Jackson
Consultants: Niamh Nic Daeid and Paul Knepper
Editor: Anna Southgate
Designer: Dave Jones
Proofreader: Richard Beatty

Dedicated to Caspian & Iona

Distributed in the U.S. and Canada by Macmillan,
120 Broadway, New York, NY 10271

EU representative: 1st Floor, The Liffey Trust Centre,
117-126 Sheriff Street Upper, Dublin 1 D01 YC43

Library of Congress Cataloging-in-Publication Data has been applied for.

ISBN: 978-0-7534-7885-1 (Hardcover)
ISBN: 978-0-7534-7886-8 (Paperback)

Kingfisher books are available for special promotions and premiums.
For details contact: Special Markets Department, Macmillan, 120 Broadway,
New York, NY 10271

For more information, please visit www.kingfisherbooks.com

Printed in China
9 8 7 6 5 4 3 2 1
1TR/0323/WKT/RV/128MA

MIX
Paper | Supporting
responsible forestry
FSC® C116313

CONTENTS

Introduction
Dr. Edmond Locard

"Every contact leaves a trace." That is the foundation of crime scene investigation, and it was me who said it, in France, way back in 1910. What I'm saying is that no crime occurs without the people involved leaving traces at the scene—minute specks and flecks of materials and substances. They also take traces with them when they leave. Studying tiny traces can help solve big mysteries. I was the first person to speak about this.

I came up with systems for putting all the traces together, and forensic science grew from there. I made it my business to collect traces of all kinds—blood, fingerprints, and fibers—and then spent time figuring out which ones were important. I didn't come up with the word "forensic"; that has roots that go back to Roman times, when a suspect and accuser argued their case in the public square, or "forum." Today the public investigation of a crime is solved in a courtroom and forensic science is the presentation of science in front of *that* forum. Come on, let's find out more.

Chapter 1
Crimes "R" Us

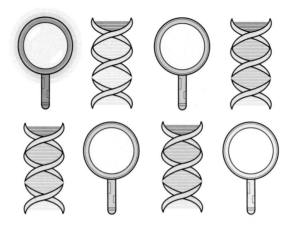

Stay away from us! We're nothing but trouble. We take stuff that isn't ours and give nothing back in return. We don't even care who loses out in the process. As long as we get what we came for, we're happy, and we have a habit of coming back for more. We have no interest in justice—other people can worry about that. And we won't stop until we're made to stop by law-enforcement types like the Super Sleuths! We often play cat and mouse with those detective types in the hope that we'll get away with our crimes.

Theft

Counterfeiting

Fraud

Forgery

Cyber Crime

Arson

Murder

Theft

■ Crimes "R" Us

☀ This light-fingered lifter is all take, take, take
☀ Leaves nothing but a trail of traces
☀ Is put off by bright lights, cameras, and alarms

What's mine is mine, and what's yours is mine too! That's the way I look at it. If I see something I want, I just take it. I'm a common crime, and I almost always leave traces for the Crime Scene Crew to collect.

When I go inside people's homes, you can call me burglary. I aim to target empty houses, preferably those without alarms, locks, and security lights. I make a lot of mess as I break in and look around—it's difficult not to leave evidence that gives me away. When I steal things like clothes, jewelry, or food from stores, I'm known as shoplifting. I'm often left holding stolen goods and risk being caught red-handed! I hate security! It slows me down—products sometimes have tags that sound an alarm, and there are cameras everywhere!

● Taking something is called theft if you intend never to give it back
● Biggest theft ever: $1 billion taken from the Central Bank of Iraq, 2003
● In the United States there is a burglary every 31 seconds

Theft

Counterfeiting

■ Crimes "R" Us

✳ This cheater cashes in on imitation money
✳ Makes cheap copies of paper money as a shortcut to riches
✳ A real fake that is seldom as good as it thinks it is

I make fake cash that can be used just like real money. Coins aren't worth much, and they're expensive to make, so I favor paper money. That might sound rich coming from me, but this caper is not as easy as it sounds.

In the U.S., when making banknotes, the U.S. Bureau of Engraving and Printing employs all sorts of tricks to catch me out. For example, it uses raised printing that has a certain feel in your fingers—you just know when it's not the real thing. Plus, notes are printed with intricate designs that are hard to copy, sometimes using color-shifting inks. Concealed in the patterns are watermarks and notes of $5 or more have a security thread that glows blue, orange, green, yellow, or pink depending on their value. Hmmm, it's a pretty tall order to make a fake, after all!

● The U.S. Secret Service was originally created in 1865 to fight counterfeiters
● Countries change their coins and bills regularly to foil counterfeiters
● U.S. paper money is actually made of a blend of cotton and linen

Counterfeiting

Fraud

■ Crimes "R" Us

☀ A daylight robber who uses fake documents to steal money
☀ This quiet con artist finds ways to trick the system
☀ Works in plain sight but is sometimes hard to see

I'm not what I seem—that's the point. I'm a sly trickster who cheats the system. For example, I find ways to steal money by pretending to be someone I'm not. Forgery and Cyber Crime are close friends of mine, as I use fake documents or stolen banking information to transfer someone else's funds to secret accounts. Everything looks normal, so I'm a hard crime to spot.

Fraud

● In the U.S. more than two million people are affected by fraud each year
● About $5 trillion is stolen through fraud every year in the United States
● Two-factor authentication (a double security check) helps block fraudsters

Forgery

Crimes "R" Us ■

* A copycat who likes a fake better than the real thing
* This ID crook creates false identities out of the blue
* Makes replicas of artworks to sell to hapless collectors

Forgery

I'm a crime that fakes it to make it. Perhaps my simplest trick is to change the name of the payee on a check. I also work with Fraud to create false documents like passports and driver's licenses. Sometimes I make copies of famous artworks, or luxury branded goods like handbags and perfume, to sell as the real deal. Buyer beware, I say!

● More than 3 percent of branded products sold are actually forgeries
● A Leonardo da Vinci painting sold in 2017 for $450 million; experts think it's a fake
● To outwit forgers, a microchip in a passport contains the owner's biometric data

Cyber Crime

■ Crimes "R" Us

✳ This nerd gone bad uses their computing powers for ill
✳ Sneaks spying software onto computers to steal secrets
✳ Can dispatch an entire army of bots to bring down big stings

A.k.a. hacking, my kind of crime is slick clicks and secret software. My aim is to take control of your computer, and I work in many different ways. I might cause trouble by infecting a machine with a virus that clogs up the Internet, for example. Or perhaps I'll create an army of infected computers (a botnet) that hacks into important computer systems like those of banks and news channels.

But watch out for emails or texts that tell you to fix your device or reset services. That might just be me phishing! Pretending to be someone else, I'll tell you to click on a link to set things right, while actually using it to install malware (a program that allows me to steal passwords and top-secret documents) or ransomware (which stops you from accessing your computer until you pay me some money).

● One in three U.S. homes has a computer with malware on it
● As many as 600,000 social media accounts are hacked every day
● A 2011 hack of company emails handled by Epsilon cost $4 billion to fix

Cyber Crime

Arson
■ Crimes "R" Us

☀ A hot, fiery marauder that can run out of control
☀ This fire starter can easily kill by mistake
☀ Often leaves plenty of clues among the ashes

I'm a truly terrifying and very serious crime that often gets way out of control. I'm a really bad idea that starts by setting fire to a building. I might be used to scare or threaten someone. Or perhaps I'll team up with Fraud to profit from an insurance claim. Sometimes I'm just a thoughtless act perpetrated in the hope of creating some excitement. The problem is, once I've started, I don't know when to stop. I spread rapidly and often end up doing terrible damage—someone might even be killed.

Try me just once and you'll end up in jail. Even if I have burned away everything, I always leave clues. The Lab Bench Bunch can tell which fuel I used to get the flames going, and the Super Sleuths will be looking for those chemicals elsewhere. I'm feeling the heat right now!

● Eight out of ten arsonists are male, and half of them are children
● In the U.S., one arsonist destroyed more than 300 buildings over a period of 30 years
● In 2017/18, half of the fires in the United Kingdom were due to arson

Arson

Murder

■ Crimes "R" Us

※ A crime that sees one person take the life of another person
※ The Super Sleuths never give up chasing this villain
※ Gets a one-way ticket to prison that can last a lifetime

I'm as serious as crime gets—someone dies because of me, and their death is wholly intentional. The punishment for my crime is a life in prison, spending many years behind bars.

You might know me as homicide. The worst kind of homicide is when there is a definite intention for the victim to die. In some cases, my actions are planned out before the crime takes place. In other cases, a person's life is lost as another crime—say, Theft or Arson—is playing out. But my wrongdoing is more complex than that. For example, one person might kill another in the heat of the moment. Or someone might behave recklessly but never mean to kill. In these cases, my crime is often called manslaughter. They are still serious crimes—someone has lost a life, after all—but the punishment tends to be less severe.

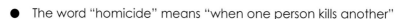

● The word "homicide" means "when one person kills another"
● Country with highest murder rate: El Salvador
● Country with lowest murder rate: Japan

Murder

Chapter 2
The Crime Scene Crew

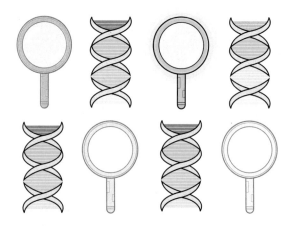

A crime scene holds many traces and clues, so we need to tread very carefully. Shoe Print and Fingerprint reveal a person's presence. Photography keeps a close account of what we find—from specks of blood to flecks of paint—recording where these traces are in relation to other things at the scene. But it's not for us to decide what any of this means. That's a job for Detective once the Lab Bench Bunch have examined our helpful haul. So stay out of our way, please. We'll be here for as long as it takes; this crime scene won't investigate itself.

Protective
Clothing

Photography

CSI Kit

DNA Collection

Fingerprint

Shoe Print and
Tire Track

Blood Spatter

Protective Clothing

※ An outer layer that keeps confusion to a minimum
※ This simple coverall keeps the crime scene crew safe
※ A must for investigators—those without, keep out

When investigating a crime scene, it is crucial only to collect traces connected to the crime. I make sure unwanted material does not get in to cause confusion. I'm a simple but effective outer covering: a full body suit —usually white in color— with a hood to keep hair in place and covers for shoes. Final touches are gloves and a face mask. Suit up, we're going in!

Protective Clothing

● Crime scene suits are made of a lightweight, breathable plastic material
● An investigator's shoe covers are sometimes collected and kept as evidence
● Special clothing keeps investigators safe from toxins at the scene

The Crime Scene Crew

* This sharp-eyed type documents a crime scene
* Takes photographs of what lies where following a crime
* Used in court to show the crime scene to the jury

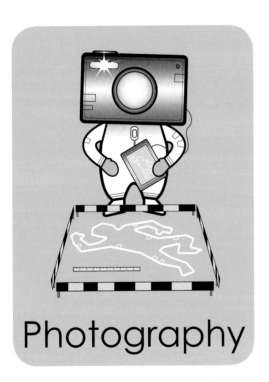

Photography

A picture tells a thousand words, and I have plenty to say about a crime scene. I record every trace uncovered by the Crime Scene Crew, snapping images from all angles to show exactly where a trace was found. I add tags and flags to identify each trace and might use a ruler beside an object to show its size. Sometimes I use different types of light to highlight certain features.

* Swiss scientist R.A. Reiss was a pioneer of forensic photography
* Infrared and ultraviolet photos are used to reveal body fluids and fingerprints
* Photographers sometimes use flash fill to highlight details in shadowy areas

CSI Kit

■ The Crime Scene Crew

☀ CSI stands for **c**rime **s**cene **i**nvestigation
☀ This well-equipped crew member gets an investigation going
☀ Includes containers for weapons, blood, hair, and other samples

As soon as Protective Clothing is on and Photography has recorded the untouched scene, it's time for me to get to work. My kit can handle just about anything found here. Evidence containers are extremely important: hard boxes for weapons, plastic bags and tubes for smaller items. Anything can be important—a letter, a phone, or a strand of hair. I even inspect the contents of trash cans.

I like to start my search at the edge of a room and work toward the middle. That way nothing gets missed. I use a notepad to record everything I do and everything I collect. I write labels for containers, saying what's inside, and I sign and date the labels. I seal up the containers at the scene. I do absolutely everything with the utmost care and attention. Justice is depending on it.

● All evidence taken from a crime scene is very carefully logged
● Signing and dating each item starts a process called the continuity of evidence
● Every collected item is accounted for from the crime scene to the courtroom

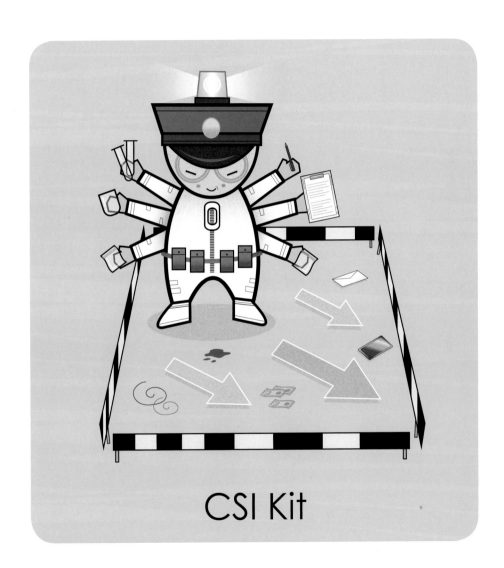

CSI Kit

DNA Collection
The Crime Scene Crew

* This clean-cut swab captures DNA . . . but whose is it?
* Soaks up samples of body fluids for analysis in the lab
* Can be used to find a match with a known suspect

One of the most important traces at a crime scene is deoxyribonucleic acid—that's DNA to you and me! This complex chemical holds the instruction codes for building a human body. Everyone has it, and everyone's DNA is unique to them (unless they happen to have an identical twin, that is). If the DNA I collect at a crime scene matches that of a known suspect, I might have found a criminal!

Whether it's a strand of hair, a glass with a lip smear, or snot on a tissue, I bag it up carefully for the lab. I also take the DNA of suspects, victims, and witnesses—a simple swab from inside the mouth is enough. During a struggle or fight, flakes of skin or spots of blood get lodged under fingernails. I collect those too. Then it's off to the Lab Bench Bunch and DNA Profiling to try to establish whose DNA I've found.

● Investigators have about 96 hours to collect DNA before it breaks up
● DNA samples are stored in a freezer to stop them from degrading
● A DNA sample can reveal a suspect's sex but not their hair or skin color

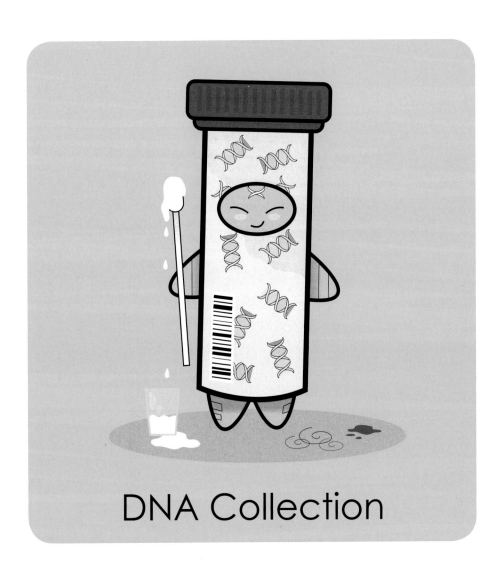

DNA Collection

Fingerprint
The Crime Scene Crew

* A tip-off for investigators searching a crime scene
* An old and dusty technique from the early days of CSI
* Shows up as smudges that reveal who touched what

I'm the oldest member of the Crime Scene Crew, a forensic science technique with more than 130 years of experience. Every fleshy fingertip has a pattern of ridges that form swirls and loops. These patterns vary from person to person, and the chances of two people having the same pattern on their fingertips are really, really small.

Fingers leave traces of sweaty and fatty materials that show up with a dusting of powder or some other chemical. I might be a partial or complete finger mark, or even a whole hand mark. Transferred to a plastic sheet, I head back to the lab for analysis. Computer imaging detects the features in a finger mark and compares them to prints collected from suspects and victims. I may be old, but I can still make all the difference in identifying the bad guys.

* Identical twins share identical DNA but have different fingerprints
* The chance of two people having identical fingerprints is 1 in 64 billion
* The FBI has 77 million sets of fingerprints on record

Fingerprint

Shoe Print and Tire Track

■ The Crime Scene Crew

☀ The search is on for marks left by shoes and tires
☀ This grounded pair of sleuths help show the way
☀ Eyes down: the floor is where their evidence lies

Clues often lie underfoot, so please be careful where you stand. Marks left by shoes show what a suspect was wearing on their feet. Any soil or dirt left inside might reveal where they walked before arriving at the scene. Everyone walks in a different way, wearing down their shoes' soles in a particular pattern. If a crime scene pattern matches that of a suspect's soles, Detective needs to know about it!

The Crime Scene Crew can learn a lot from Tire Track, including the direction in which a vehicle traveled to and from a crime scene. Car and bike tires wear down in different places over time. So not only does Tire Track indicate the size and make of a vehicle used at a crime scene, it can even help identify the exact vehicle.

● Investigators take casts of sole patterns from shoe prints left in mud and soil
● The size of a shoe can help with figuring out how tall a suspect might be
● To check tire tracks, investigators ink up a vehicle's tires and drive over paper

Shoe Print and Tire Track

Blood Spatter
■ The Crime Scene Crew

✳ This ruddy type explains patterns made by spilled blood
✳ The shapes and sizes of droplets give a lot away
✳ Reveals gruesome details by making a splash

At times, members of the Crime Scene Crew must investigate gruesome events in which people have been hurt or killed. First things first: victims always get urgent treatment—nothing else is more important. But after that, I can be useful by helping to explain what happened.

I am the pattern that blood makes when it spreads from a wound. I indicate the type of weapon used and whether a victim was standing up at the time of the attack (big drips suggest the blood has fallen a long way). Patterns on walls and floors show which direction the blood came from and might reveal something about the victim's movement around the scene. It's a nasty aspect of detection, but I color in the missing parts of the picture so the Super Sleuths can figure out what happened in this horrible crime.

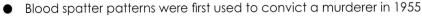

● Blood spatter patterns were first used to convict a murderer in 1955
● Investigators examine both the size and the shape of a blood spot
● Various technologies help reveal blood stains invisible to the naked eye

Blood Spatter

Chapter 3
The Lab Bench Bunch

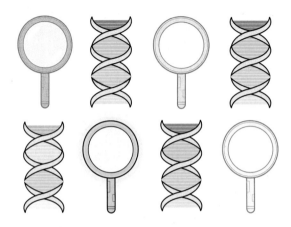

Welcome to the back room! Working away from the public glare, and on behalf of the courts, we do the most important work in solving crime. Sure, it takes a lot of time and patience, but we get results. Our role is to examine the traces collected by the Crime Scene Crew. We work with chemicals and high-tech systems to establish the bare facts. The findings of our tests give an indication as to whether a suspect committed the crime or not. Based on our efforts, the Super Sleuths can go catch who dunnit, while letting the innocent go free.

Chemical
Analysis

Microscopic
Analysis

Ballistics

DNA Profiling

Autopsy

Forensic
Entomology

Facial
Recognition

Voice
Recognition

Chemical Analysis

■ The Lab Bench Bunch

☀ This science sleuth breaks down crime scene clues
☀ Collects chemical signatures from the substances found
☀ Narrows down the search for investigating officers

Bubble, bubble, toil, it's no trouble. I work hard in the lab, running tests on substances collected by the Crime Scene Crew. The chemical makeup of flecks of paint, fragments of soil, or smears of oil could link the people involved in a crime with other places or things.

I use high-tech gizmos to analyze the chemicals found in traces from a crime scene or recovered from suspects and victims. Some machines separate chemical mixtures to pinpoint what they contain. Others help me identify fibers, paint, and glass fragments. I'm kept busy. Bench buddy Ballistics needs my help to understand what type of gunpowder was used in a gun. Fire Investigator wants to know what fuel was lit to start a fire. I can even help good old Fingerprint show what the suspect had for lunch!

● The first forensic chemists from the 1830s were searching for poisons
● Spectrometry identifies materials by shining light of different wavelengths on them
● Mass spectrometers separate chemicals based on differences in weight

Chemical Analysis

Microscopic Analysis

The Lab Bench Bunch

✳ This wide-eyed observer likes to take a closer look
✳ Lends a lens to reveal what's what
✳ Reveals teeny-tiny details that can make or break a case

Make some room—I'm here to take a better look at everything. I get real close to the evidence in the hope that I'll find hidden information. I examine bullets for telltale patterns, I help identify germs and bugs living in human remains, and I can see details in fibers or paint that are invisible to the naked eye.

I make use of different kinds of light, switching colors and swinging in at angles to show the finest details, like the impressions left on a pad of paper to identify different types of pens. I'm also very important in the study of fibers, helping to identify where they are from—a carpet, a car seat, or clothes, perhaps? Give me a good look at the tips and I can even tell you if they were cut, snapped, or stretched. The truth is in the tiny details.

● Residual particles from gunshots can be less than 1/100 mm wide
● A pollen grain can link an item to the place where the plant it came from grows
● The tiniest traces of blood and other fluids can be seen under a microscope

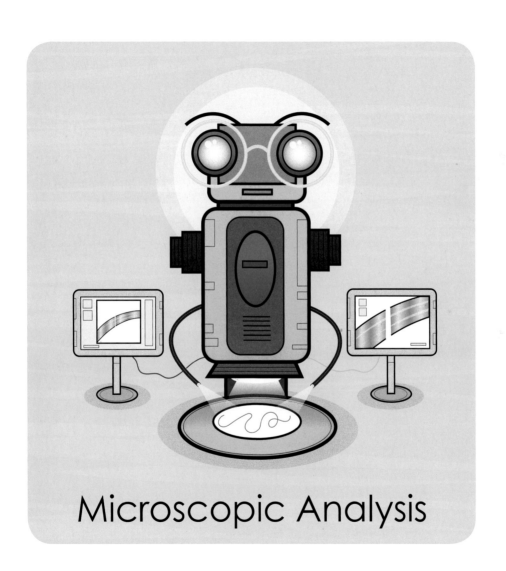

Microscopic Analysis

Ballistics

■ The Lab Bench Bunch

☀ This weapons expert provides bulletproof evidence
☀ Tests guns and bullets to link shots to possible shooters
☀ Checks the guns of criminals and police officers alike

Called in when a gun is fired during a crime, I'm interested in the type of gun used, where it was fired from, and the path the bullet took. When several people start shooting, things can get very confused, but my information can help piece together which gun was used and where the bullet was headed. It's then up to Detective to figure out why.

First I find where a bullet has ended up. Then I try to trace its flight path back to the place it was fired from. Every gun leaves scratches and dents on a bullet as it travels down the barrel. I'll need Microscopic Analysis to show these marks more clearly. I test-fire each gun to find similarities and differences between the test-fired bullets and bullets from the crime scene. This way, I might be able to identify which gun fired which bullet. That's half the battle won.

● Ballistics is the study of how any object—not just bullets—travels through the air
● The first murder solved by ballistics evidence was in London, England, in 1835
● Every gun made for sale in the last 50 years has a serial number to identify it

Ballistics

DNA Profiling

■ The Lab Bench Bunch

* This genetic genius creates a DNA ID
* Builds a profile of samples taken from a crime scene
* Uses DNA features to identify who was there

Stop pointing, Fingerprint, and step aside, Shoe Print! I'm the real-deal revolutionary in fighting crime. Thanks to DNA Collection, I can turn a crime scene sample into a kind of genetic fingerprint. Let me explain how I do it.

First I extract parts of DNA taken from samples collected at the crime scene. Then I compare them with extracts of DNA taken from suspects or victims. I don't need to decode every gene. Instead, I find places in the DNA that repeat over and over—everyone has these repeating places, as their DNA comes from their mom and dad. My profiles give a pattern like a set of thick and thin bars, which is different for each person (except for identical twins, of course). It's important work that could mean iron bars for the person whose profile I find.

● DNA profiling was invented in 1984
● In 1988 a murderer was identified by crime scene DNA for the first time
● DNA evidence has also been used to reverse wrongful convictions

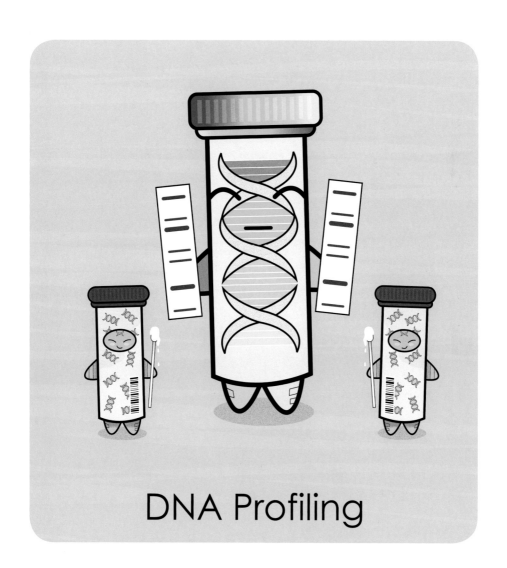

DNA Profiling

Autopsy
The Lab Bench Bunch

✳ This medical investigator always makes the cut
✳ Looks inside and out to find the cause and time of death
✳ Writes a final chapter in the search for a murderer

There is a silent witness to every fatality, including Murder: a dead body. Even though it cannot speak, a body contains a lot of information about what happened, and I'm the one to bring it to the surface.

Performed by Forensic Pathologist, I start with a close inspection of the body, looking for wounds, cuts, and bruises that reveal how this person died. Next I'll look deeper, cutting into the body to check the brain and other organs. These might show that death had a natural cause. Other features of a body, such as its color or smell, might help establish the time of death. Chemical Analysis is called in to check for poisons, while Microscopic Analysis finds hidden traces that show if the body has been moved from place to place. The dead do talk—but only to me.

● Julius Caesar had an autopsy after being murdered in 44 BC
● *Liver mortis*, the way blood settles, shows a body's position after death
● Experts on the causes of death are called pathologists

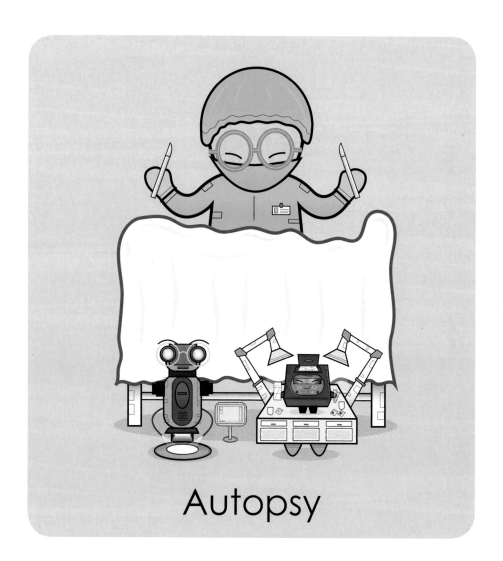

Autopsy

Forensic Entomology

The Lab Bench Bunch

* An expert on the life cycles of insects
* Particularly familiar with flies and beetles
* Examines eggs and larvae to give time and place of death

This might seem gruesome to you, but nature has an amazing way of helping me guide The Super Sleuths in their work. You see, when a dead body starts to decompose, insects move in to feed on it. This is all perfectly natural and makes sense for their survival.

Different insects feed on dead animals, laying their eggs in or on the body. Some move in right after death, while others prefer older remains. Depending on what kind of critter is crawling around at the time a body is found, I can figure out how long ago that person died—it could be days, weeks, or even months. And because insects favor different habitats, from swamps to forests to deserts, I might be able to tell where a person died and whether their body was moved. My insect informers will let me know.

- Entomology is the study of insects
- Insects lay their eggs in dead bodies so their larvae have food after hatching
- The poop of maggots might contain traces of poisons involved in a death

Forensic Entomology

Facial Recognition

The Lab Bench Bunch

* A scan fan that works face to face
* Converts a person's face into a set of measurements
* Helpful in finding suspects in and around a crime scene

Snap! That's my game—matching a person of interest to pictures of faces caught on camera. I work by dividing facial features into a set of shapes and measurements that can be matched with any other face in the crowd. Detective uses me to try to identify suspects loitering at the time of a crime. I'm not accurate, however, and my evidence rarely shows up in court.

Facial Recognition

- Some say that facial recognition systems should not be watching public streets
- In tests, the system is wrong less than 1 percent of the time
- Mistakes and mismatches are more common in real situations than in tests

Voice Recognition

The Lab Bench Bunch

- ☀ A noise lover who likes to listen to others talking
- ☀ This sound fellow picks out voice features
- ☀ Helps identify who's who in audio evidence

Voice
Recognition

The sound of a person's voice can reveal a profile of the features of their speech. Working with phone calls and other recordings taken from crime scenes and individuals, I break words down to find a telltale sound signature that might identify a suspect or victim. Quality of recording is key here. Impersonators and fakers beware—you won't fool me easily!

- ● Saves time by searching automatically for a suspect's voice in recordings
- ● Every voice can be represented as a unique chart called a voice spectrograph
- ● 1987 saw the first murder conviction in which voice recognition played a part

Chapter 4
The Super Sleuths

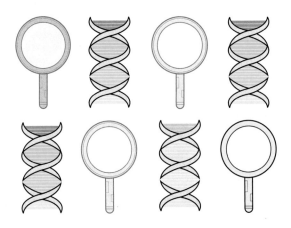

OK, gather round. This is the situation. You've heard about the hard work done down at the crime scene and back at the lab? Well, we're the forensic specialists who head out into the field (and sometimes under it) to investigate a crime further. It's our goal to build up a case and gather enough evidence to present to the court so that a jury can decide whether a suspect is guilty or innocent. Each investigation is run according to our expertise, and we work closely with the other teams to do our part. What? Now's the time? Well, let's get out there then!

Detective

Forensic
Pathologist

Forensic
Anthropologist

Forensic
Archaeologist

Fire
Investigator

Forensic Computer
Analyst

Detective
The Super Sleuths

* The police officer leading the charge against criminals
* This head honcho hunts down perpetrators
* Crooks can't escape this clued-up crime fighter

Who am I? Questions, questions—I'll do the asking, thank you! I'm the chief investigator. I rely on my team to give me the clues, and then I piece the big picture together. Some crimes are open-and-shut cases; it's clear who did what from the moment The Crime Scene Crew arrives. But there are also times when I need to detect the truth.

I'll form a theory about what happened and who did it, but can I find enough evidence for the prosecutor to prove it in court? I start with motive, means, and opportunity: Why was the crime committed? Who had the ability to carry it out? And when did they have the chance to break bad? I'm famous for getting a hunch: that feeling that something just isn't right. I'll follow the clues until the criminal is in custody. Case closed!

● Before the days of professional police, "thieftakers" were paid to solve crimes
● The word "detective" first appeared in 1843
● Detectives are trained to investigate crimes from all angles

Detective

Forensic Pathologist
The Super Sleuths

☀ Examines the body of a person who dies unexpectedly
☀ Takes charge of an investigation into the cause of death
☀ Also on hand to record medical facts in nondeadly crimes

I'm brought in when there has been an unexpected or suspicious death. No one must touch a body until I arrive on the scene. Don't confuse me with a forensic physician, though. This is someone who cares for people that get hurt during a crime, treating and recording their injuries. No, I only work with the dead.

I'm a doctor as well as a Super Sleuth, so I give clever Detective an idea about the possible time and cause of death. Knowing how long ago the person may have died can help an investigation. DNA Collection and Fingerprint help identify a victim. As soon as possible, I work with Autopsy and The Lab Bench Bunch to get a more precise account of a victim's last moments. It's all in a day's (and often night's) work for me!

● Pathology is a wide medical field that focuses on the study of disease
● There are around 500 full-time forensic pathologists in the United States
● A forensic pathologist analyzes crime scenes as well as bodies

Forensic Pathologist

Forensic Anthropologist

The Super Sleuths

* An expert in bones and burial
* Provides a biological identity from skeletal remains
* Sometimes called in for crimes long lost but not forgotten

I get down to the bare bones of a crime—literally, as I'm an expert in skeletal remains. I'm on hand when a body is found buried where it shouldn't be, or if only part of a body is discovered, or when a body is burned by fire. I'm able to tell if the remains are from a man, woman, girl, or boy, whether the person was sick or healthy, and whether their injuries are natural or not.

Sometimes I'm asked to piece together a picture of the past. I have helped explain acts of murder and killing played out long ago. Back then, of course, people may not have seen their violent deeds as crimes. Perhaps these were human sacrifices, executed wrongdoers, or casualties of war? Whatever the answer, time can't hide the truth.

* Anthropology literally means "the study of humans"
* American Wilton Krogman became the first forensic anthropologist in the 1940s
* Anthropologists might investigate war crimes and human rights violations

Forensic Anthropologist

Forensic Archaeologist
The Super Sleuths

✳ Examines clues dug up from below the ground
✳ Uses techniques designed for studying the past
✳ Also investigates historic crimes

The Crime Scene Crew calls on me to uncover evidence buried in the ground—be it recent or ancient. I use specialist skills to unearth the fragile remains I might find, recording the evidence as if I'm investigating an ancient tomb. Detective might use me to help catch a killer years after a crime, starting with determining the identity of a victim from bodily remains.

Forensic Archaeologist

● An archaeologist studies human civilizations of the past
● They have been working on crime scenes since the late 1970s
● They are experts in finding human-made structures hidden in the landscape

Fire Investigator

The Super Sleuths

✳ This fire-eyed operative looks for evidence among the ashes
✳ Gathers chemical evidence from fires started on purpose
✳ Provides an expert report, flame by flame

Fire Investigator

My job starts once the firefighters have beaten Arson into a smoldering wreck. An expert on fire, I use Chemical Analysis to figure out if a flammable liquid such as gasoline was used to start the fire and make it burn faster. I also examine the fire scene to determine where the fire started and how it spread. Detective relies on me to re-create the scene before it all burned down.

● Every fire is investigated to check for criminal activity
● Many fire investigators start out as firefighters
● One fire investigator in California was also an arsonist; he started 2,000 fires

Forensic Computer Analyst

The Super Sleuths

- ✸ This good geek hacks back against cyber crime
- ✸ Looks for clues stored on computers and other devices
- ✸ Rapidly becoming a feature in local crime labs

A modern crime scene reaches out of this world and into cyberspace. Digital devices hold trails of information, and I know where to look for them. The phones of suspects and victims show where they were before, during, and after the time of a crime. Their web searches hint at their intentions: "How do I rob a bank?" "Where can I get a fake ID?" Messages reveal friends and family members—maybe they know something? Payment data helps hunt down bad guys on the run.

Counterfeiting, Fraud, and Cyber Crime all leave computer clues. They know this, of course, and use encryption to keep their clues hidden. Do I know ways to crack their codes? Maybe I do, but that's my secret!

- A computer criminal is called a "black hat hacker"
- "White hat hackers" check that computer systems are secure
- The FBI launched its computer forensics team way back in 1984

Forensic Computer Analyst

Glossary

Analyze Study and observe something closely so it can be broken down into simple parts that show how it works in great detail.

Biometric data Measurements taken from a person's body, most likely their face, fingerprint, or, perhaps, voice. These measurements can be used to identify who someone is.

Cast A solid copy of an object that has left an imprint in something soft. The print is used as a mold to make the cast.

Con artist Short for "confidence artist"; someone who tricks people into giving away their money and possessions.

Custody When a person is held in a cell by the police.

DNA Short for deoxyribonucleic acid, DNA is a long molecule made up of many different chemicals chained together. The order of these chemicals creates the genetic code, or a list of instructions on how to build a body.

Encryption A complex code system that keeps messages secret.

Evidence Traces from a crime scene that can be used to explain what happened there and who did what.

Flash fill Using bright lights to produce clear photographs without any shadows.

Foil To prevent something from happening.

Insurance claim A request for money to replace something that has been broken or lost.

Justice A system that has been designed to ensure fairness.

Malware Software programs that do bad things.

Motive The reason why someone does something, especially why they commit a crime.

Perpetrator A person who commits a crime.

Phishing Using fake emails and messages to trap people into giving away secrets and money.

Replica A copy that looks very much like the real thing.

Software Programs and apps that run on computers.

Swab To take a sample of liquid; also the name for a cotton-tipped stick used to collect the sample.

Test-fire To fire a gun in safe way to check whether it works or to show what it does to bullets.

Toxin A poisonous substance.

Two-factor authentication A security system where people prove their identity twice to access a service.

Index